BOOK•VIDEO

HOT LICKS

C000224853

MARTY FRIEDMAN

EXOTIC METAL GUITAR

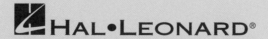

To access video visit:
www.halleonard.com/mylibrary

Enter Code
7201-2356-4864-8343

ISBN: 978-1-5400-6917-7

HAL•LEONARD®

Visit Hal Leonard Online at
www.halleonard.com

Contact us:
Hal Leonard
7777 West Bluemound Road
Milwaukee, WI 53213
Email: info@halleonard.com

In Europe, contact:
Hal Leonard Europe Limited
42 Wigmore Street
Marylebone, London, W1U 2RN
Email: info@halleonardeurope.com

In Australia, contact:
Hal Leonard Australia Pty. Ltd.
4 Lentara Court
Cheltenham, Victoria, 3192 Australia
Email: info@halleonard.com.au

BIOGRAPHY/DISCOGRAPHY

Born in Washington, D.C. in 1962, guitarist Marty Friedman took up his instrument at age 14, after attending a KISS concert. Ten years later, he joined forces with Jason Becker to form the neoclassical metal outfit Cacophony.

With the band's debut album, *Speed Metal Symphony* (Shrapnel, 1986), Friedman quickly established himself as one of the most exciting "shredders" of the era, which, in addition to bandmate Becker, also included such dexterous fret burners as Tony MacAlpine and Vinnie Moore.

In 1988, Cacophony released its second and final album, *Go Off!* The year also saw Friedman's solo debut, *Dragon's Kiss*. By this time, Friedman was not only an instrumental guitar superstar but also one with a unique voice on the instrument, which would bring him to the attention of one Dave Mustaine.

Friedman joined Megadeth in February 1990 and made his recording debut with the now legendary thrash band on their 1990 album *Rust in Peace*, on which songs like "Holy Wars… The Punishment Due," "Hangar 18," and "Tornado of Souls" featured Friedman's exotic soloing approach took center stage, propelling him beyond the shred genre and into the realm of metal guitar hero.

In a bold move, after recording five albums that sold over 10 million copies in total, Friedman announced his departure from Megadeth in December 1999.

In 2003, Friedman moved to Tokyo, Japan, where he has appeared frequently on Japanese television, collaborated with various Japanese artists, and continued to write and record solo material.

SELECT DISCOGRAPHY

Speed Metal Symphony by Cacophony (Shrapnel, 1987)

Dragon's Kiss by Marty Friedman (Shrapnel, 1988)

Rust in Peace by Megadeth (Capitol, 1990)

Countdown to Extinction by Megadeth (Capitol, 1992)

Loudspeaker by Marty Friedman (Shrapnel, 2006)

Wall of Sound by Marty Friedman (Prosthetic, 2017)

SUGGESTED LISTENING

Jason Becker *Perpetual Burn* (Shrapnel, 1988)

Steve Vai *Passion and Warfare* (Relativity/Epic, 1990)

Traditional Japanese Folk Music

CONTENTS

GUITAR NOTATION LEGEND

Guitar music can be notated three different ways: on a *musical staff*, in *tablature*, and in *rhythm slashes*.

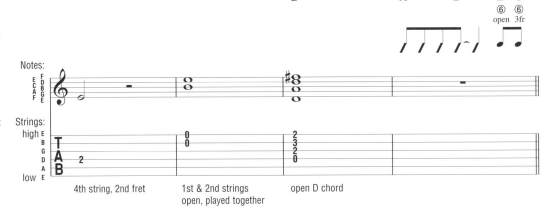

RHYTHM SLASHES are written above the staff. Strum chords in the rhythm indicated. Use the chord diagrams found at the top of the first page of the transcription for the appropriate chord voicings. Round noteheads indicate single notes.

THE MUSICAL STAFF shows pitches and rhythms and is divided by bar lines into measures. Pitches are named after the first seven letters of the alphabet.

TABLATURE graphically represents the guitar fingerboard. Each horizontal line represents a string, and each number represents a fret.

4th string, 2nd fret • 1st & 2nd strings open, played together • open D chord

Definitions for Special Guitar Notation

HALF-STEP BEND: Strike the note and bend up 1/2 step.

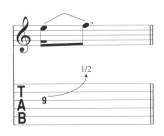

WHOLE-STEP BEND: Strike the note and bend up one step.

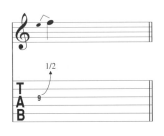

GRACE NOTE BEND: Strike the note and immediately bend up as indicated.

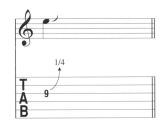

SLIGHT (MICROTONE) BEND: Strike the note and bend up 1/4 step.

BEND AND RELEASE: Strike the note and bend up as indicated, then release back to the original note. Only the first note is struck.

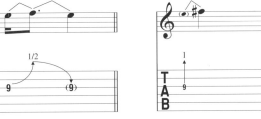

PRE-BEND: Bend the note as indicated, then strike it.

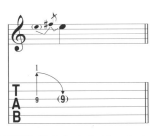

PRE-BEND AND RELEASE: Bend the note as indicated. Strike it and release the bend back to the original note.

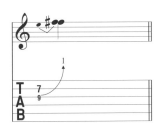

UNISON BEND: Strike the two notes simultaneously and bend the lower note up to the pitch of the higher.

VIBRATO: The string is vibrated by rapidly bending and releasing the note with the fretting hand.

WIDE VIBRATO: The pitch is varied to a greater degree by vibrating with the fretting hand.

HAMMER-ON: Strike the first (lower) note with one finger, then sound the higher note (on the same string) with another finger by fretting it without picking.

PULL-OFF: Place both fingers on the notes to be sounded. Strike the first note and without picking, pull the finger off to sound the second (lower) note.

LEGATO SLIDE: Strike the first note and then slide the same fret-hand finger up or down to the second note. The second note is not struck.

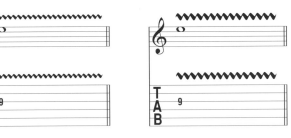

SHIFT SLIDE: Same as legato slide, except the second note is struck.

TRILL: Very rapidly alternate between the notes indicated by continuously hammering on and pulling off.

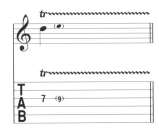

TAPPING: Hammer ("tap") the fret indicated with the pick-hand index or middle finger and pull off to the note fretted by the fret hand.

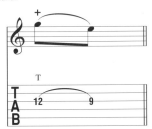

NATURAL HARMONIC: Strike the note while the fret-hand lightly touches the string directly over the fret indicated.

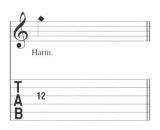

PINCH HARMONIC: The note is fretted normally and a harmonic is produced by adding the edge of the thumb or the tip of the index finger of the pick hand to the normal pick attack.

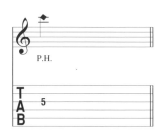

HARP HARMONIC: The note is fretted normally and a harmonic is produced by gently resting the pick hand's index finger directly above the indicated fret (in parentheses) while the pick hand's thumb or pick assists by plucking the appropriate string.

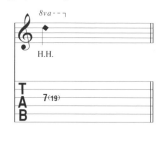

PICK SCRAPE: The edge of the pick is rubbed down (or up) the string, producing a scratchy sound.

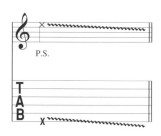

MUFFLED STRINGS: A percussive sound is produced by laying the fret hand across the string(s) without depressing, and striking them with the pick hand.

PALM MUTING: The note is partially muted by the pick hand lightly touching the string(s) just before the bridge.

RAKE: Drag the pick across the strings indicated with a single motion.

TREMOLO PICKING: The note is picked as rapidly and continuously as possible.

ARPEGGIATE: Play the notes of the chord indicated by quickly rolling them from bottom to top.

VIBRATO BAR DIVE AND RETURN: The pitch of the note or chord is dropped a specified number of steps (in rhythm), then returned to the original pitch.

VIBRATO BAR SCOOP: Depress the bar just before striking the note, then quickly release the bar.

VIBRATO BAR DIP: Strike the note and then immediately drop a specified number of steps, then release back to the original pitch.

Additional Musical Definitions

(accent)	• Accentuate note (play it louder).	
(accent)	• Accentuate note with great intensity.	
(staccato)	• Play the note short.	
	• Downstroke	
V	• Upstroke	
D.S. al Coda	• Go back to the sign (%), then play until the measure marked "*To Coda*," then skip to the section labelled "**Coda**."	
D.C. al Fine	• Go back to the beginning of the song and play until the measure marked "*Fine*" (end).	

Rhy. Fig. • Label used to recall a recurring accompaniment pattern (usually chordal).

Riff • Label used to recall composed, melodic lines (usually single notes) which recur.

Fill • Label used to identify a brief melodic figure which is to be inserted into the arrangement.

Rhy. Fill • A chordal version of a Fill.

tacet • Instrument is silent (drops out).

• Repeat measures between signs.

• When a repeated section has different endings, play the first ending only the first time and the second ending only the second time.

NOTE: Tablature numbers in parentheses mean:
    1. The note is being sustained over a system (note in standard notation is tied), or
    2. The note is sustained, but a new articulation (such as a hammer-on, pull-off, slide or vibrato) begins, or
    3. The note is a barely audible "ghost" note (note in standard notation is also in parentheses).

SECTION I: Patterns, Exercises, and Variations

Chapter 1: Patterns of Five

Example 1
(0:40)

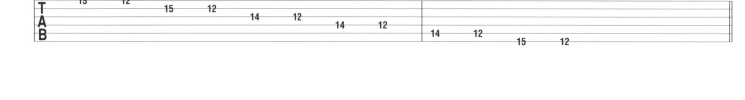

Example 2
(1:00)

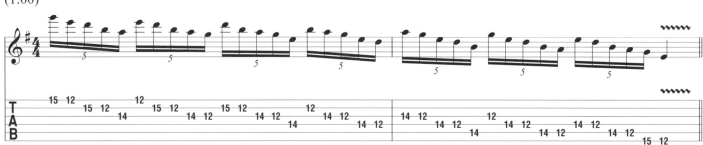

Example 3
(1:45)

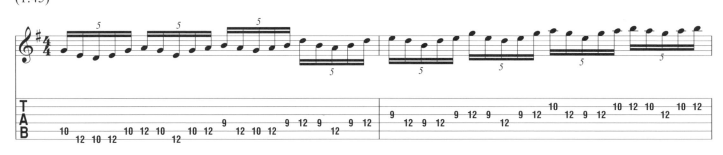

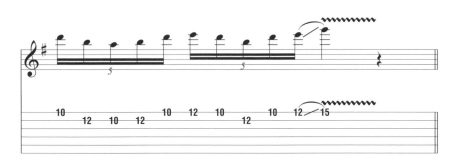

Example 4
(2:19)

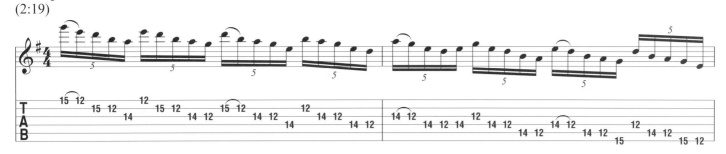

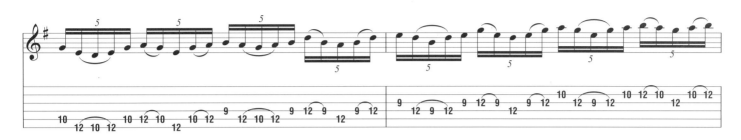

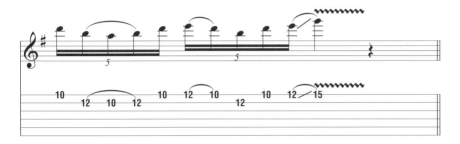

Example 5
(3:24)

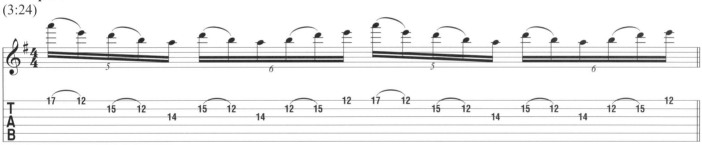

Example 6
(4:24)

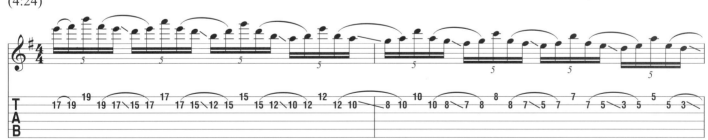

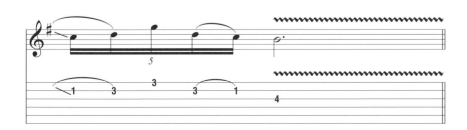

Chapter 2: Arpeggio Patterns

Example 7
(0:24)

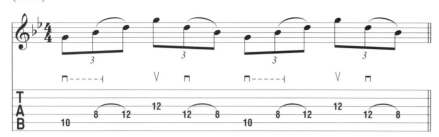

Example 8
(1:25)

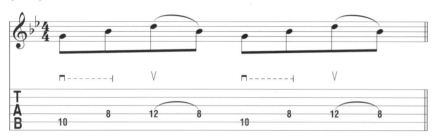

Example 9
(1:41)

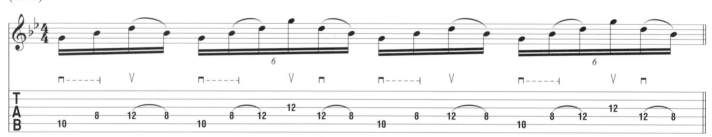

Example 10
(1:48)

Example 11
(2:09)

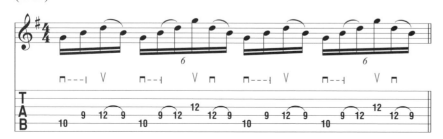

Example 12
(2:50)

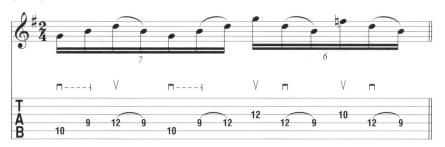

Example 13
(3:47)

Example 14
(4:26)

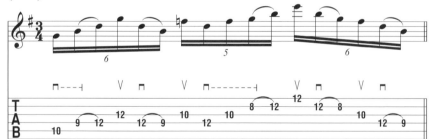

Example 15
(6:31)

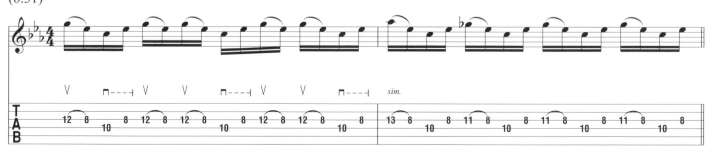

Chapter 3: Diminished Patterns

Example 16
(0:13)

Example 17
(0:30)

Example 18
(0:43)

Example 19
(1:02)

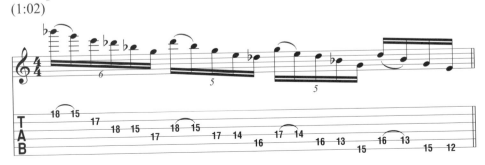

Example 20
(1:28)

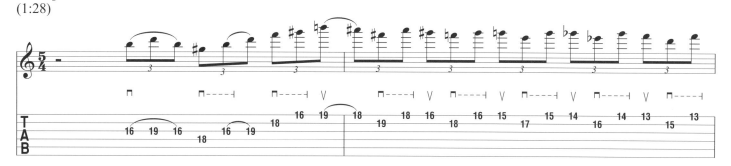

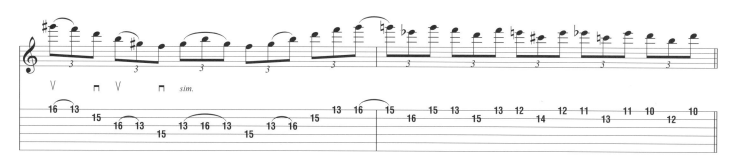

Example 21
(1:50)

Example 22
(2:27)

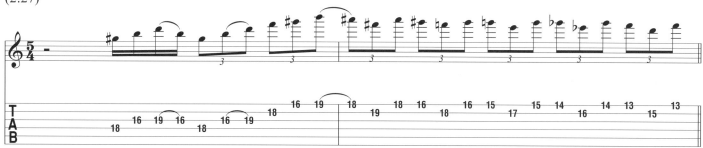

Example 23
(2:33)

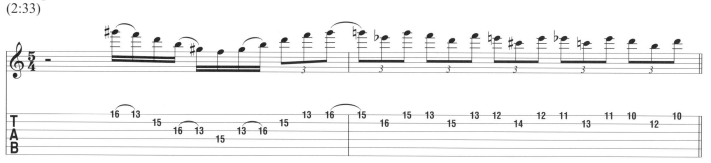

Example 24
(2:47)

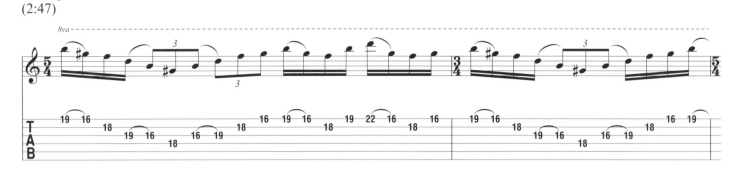

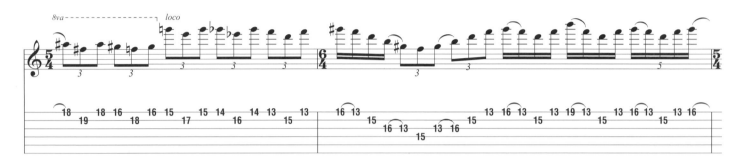

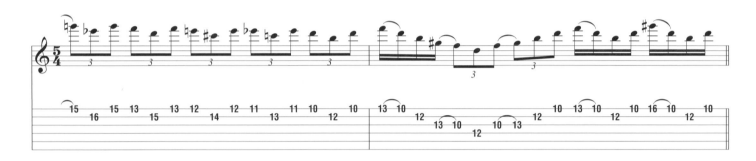

Example 25A
(4:14)

Example 25B
(4:27)

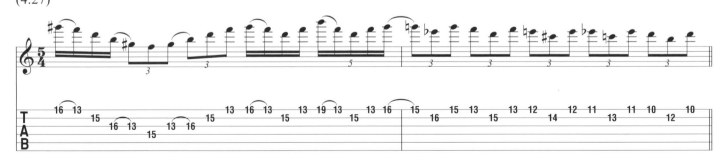

Example 25C
(4:35)

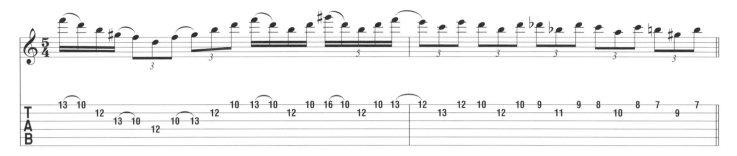

Example 25D
(4:42)

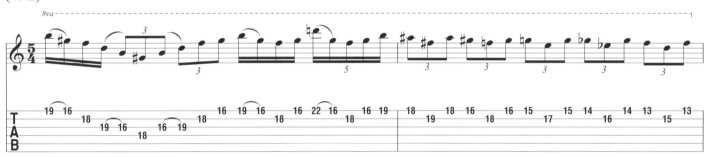

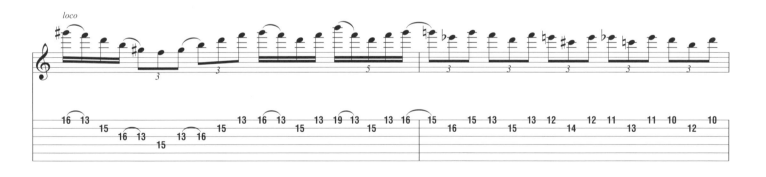

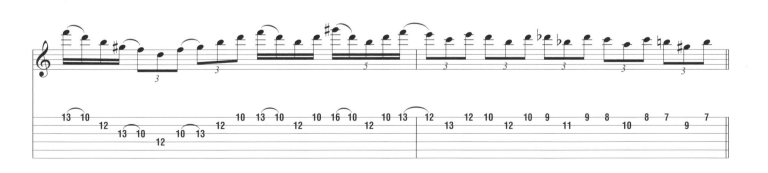

13

Chapter 4: Minor Arpeggios

Example 26
(0:36)

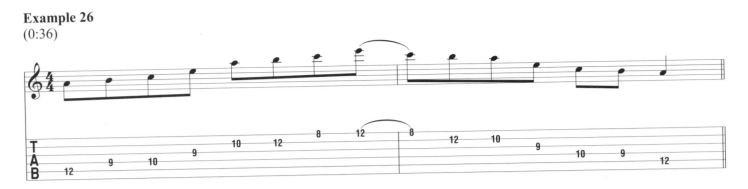

Example 27
(0:47)

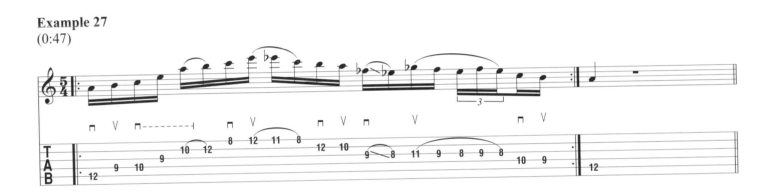

Example 28
(1:45)

Example 29
(2:05)

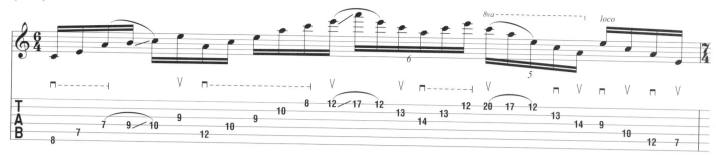

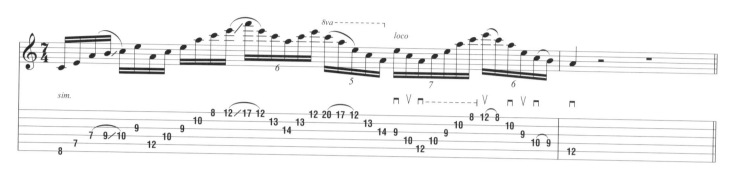

Example 30
(3:27)

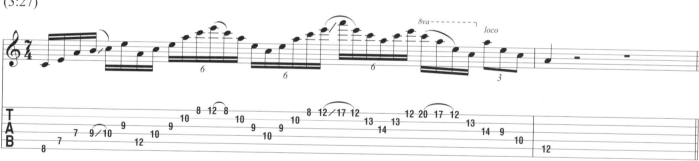

SECTION II: Exotic Playing

Chapter 5: Japanese Scale

Example 31
(0:35)

Example 32
(1:09)

Example 33
(1:23)

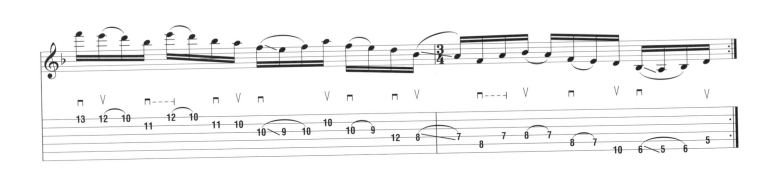

Example 34
(4:10)

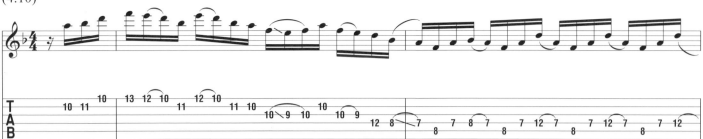

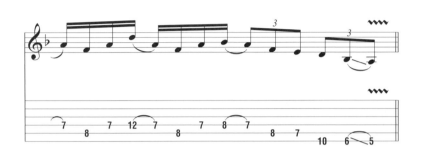

Example 35
(5:11)

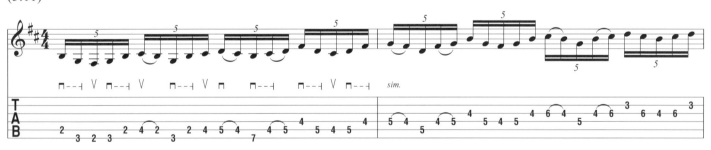

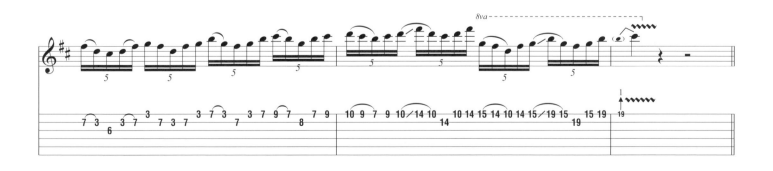

17

Chapter 6: Exotic String Bending

Example 36A
(0:23)

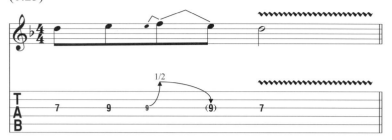

Example 36B
(0:50)

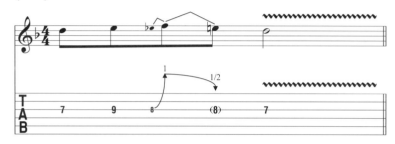

Example 37
(1:15)

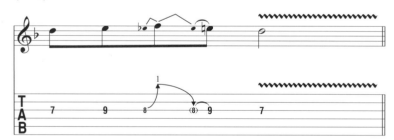

Example 38
(1:30)

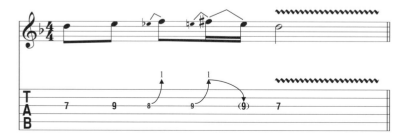

Example 39
(2:05)

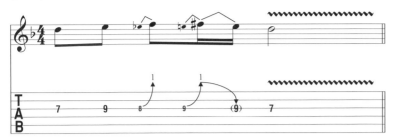

Example 40
(2:33)

Example 41
(2:48)

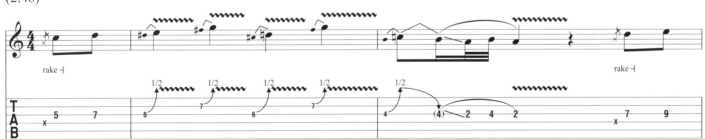

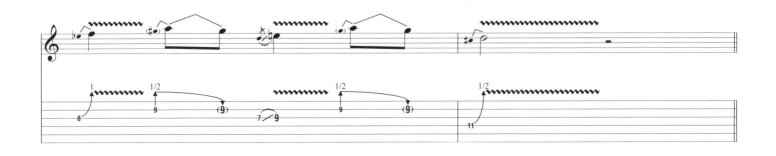

Chapter 7: Pause and Rush

Example 42
(0:29)

Example 43
(0:36)

*Played behind the beat.

Example 44
(0:59)

*Played behind the beat.

Example 45
(1:23)

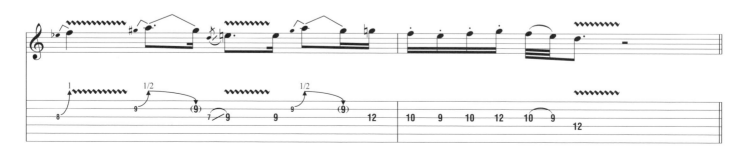

SECTION III: Soloing Approach

Chapter 8: Solo with Breakdown

Example 46
(0:46)

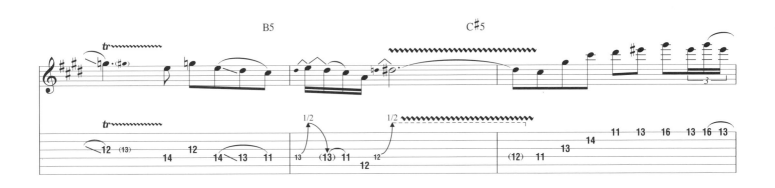

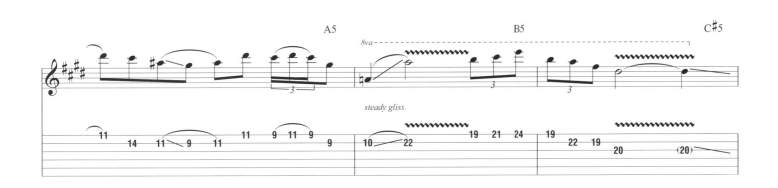

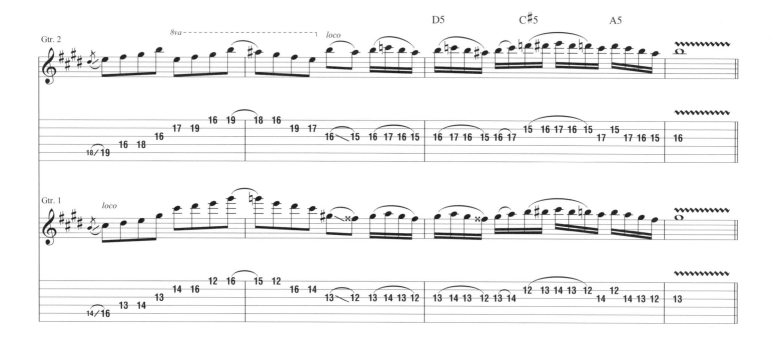

Example 47

(1:11)

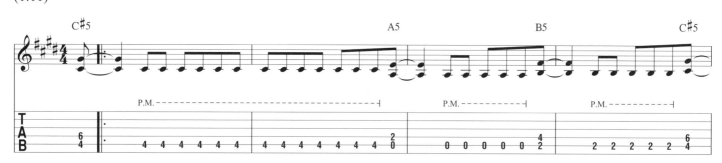

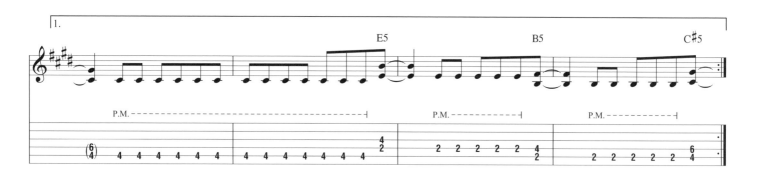

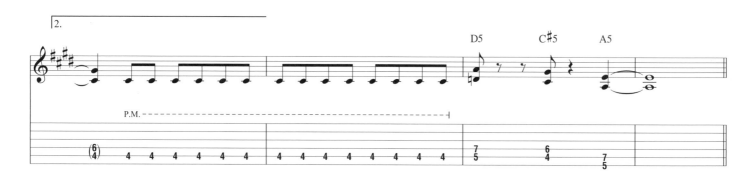

Outro

Example 48

(0:06)

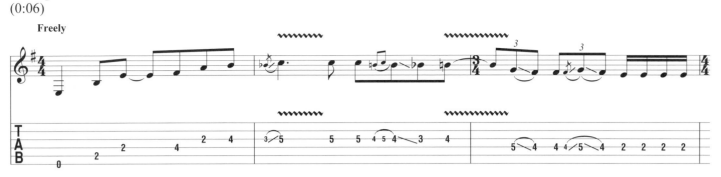

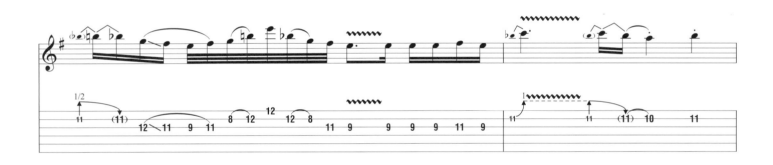
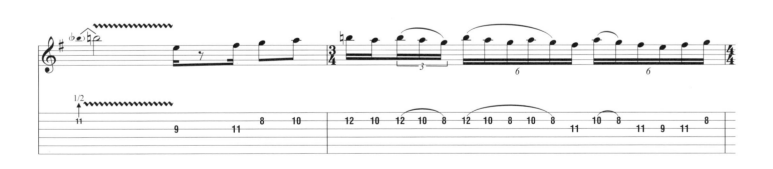
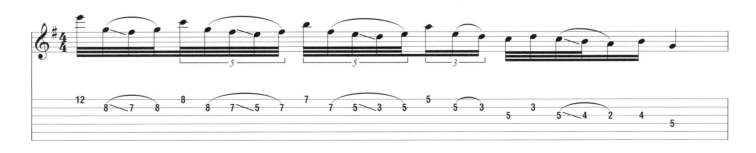

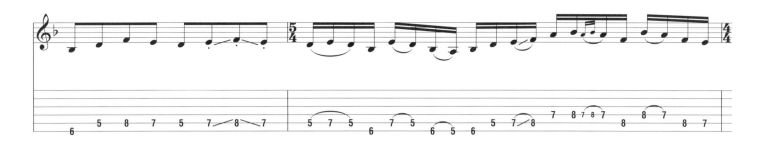
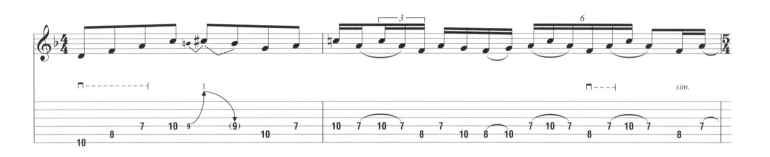
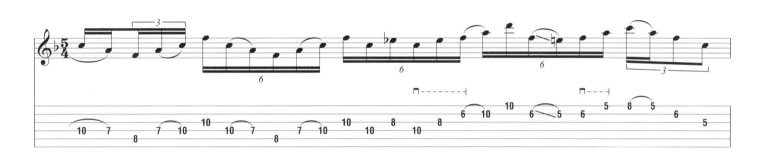
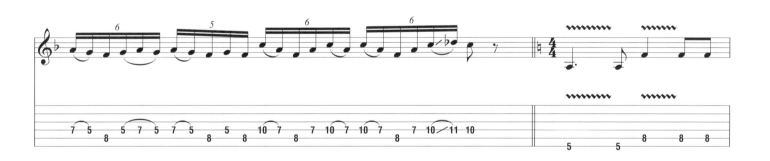

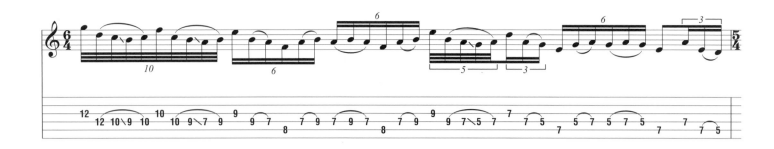

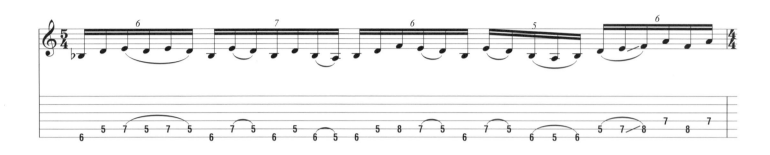

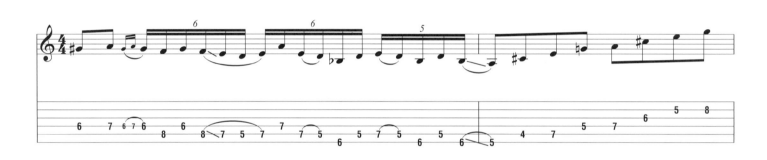

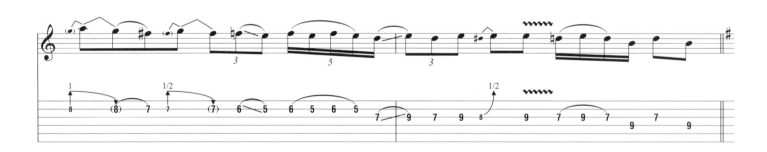

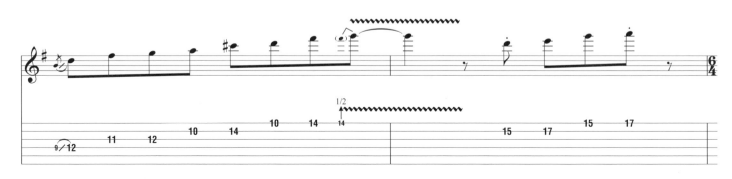

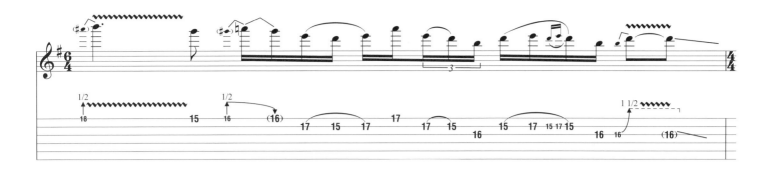
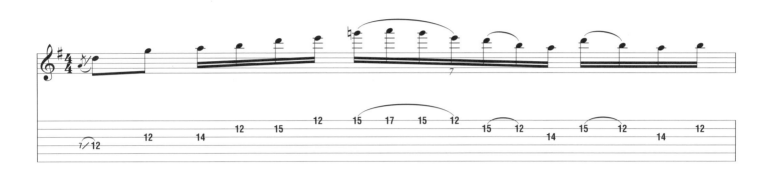
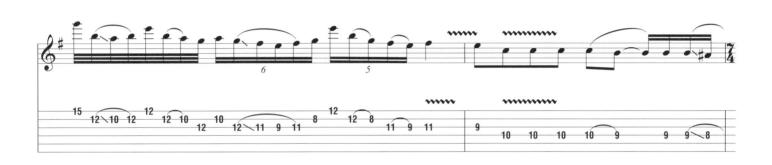

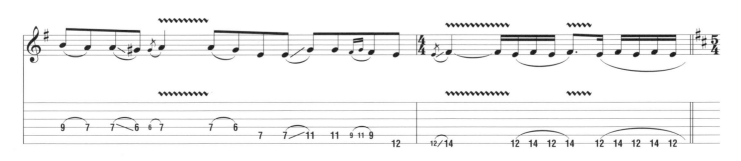

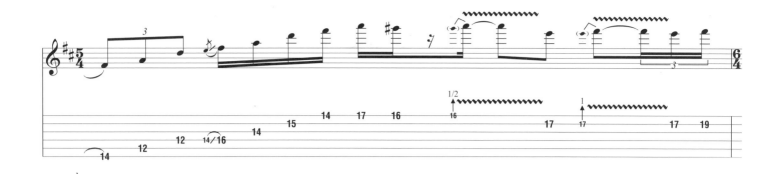

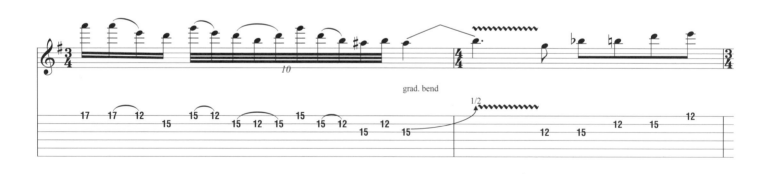

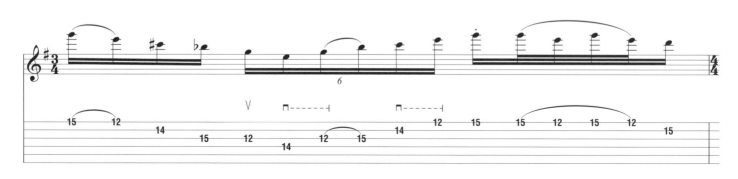

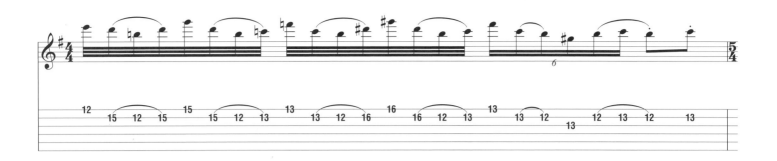

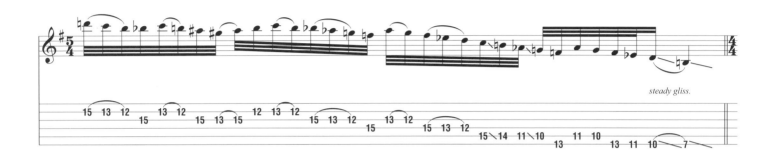

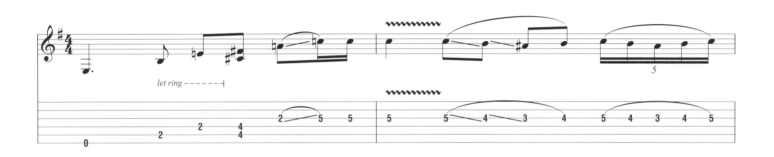

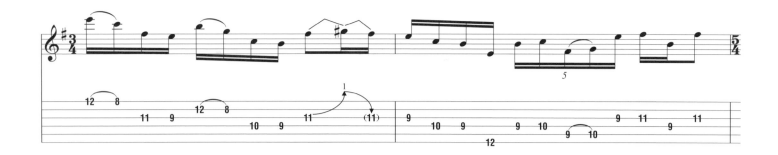

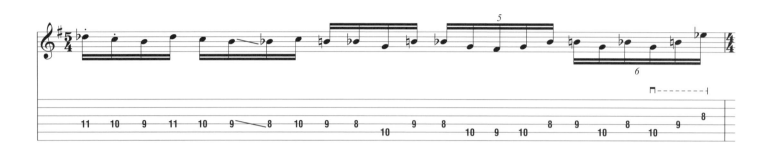

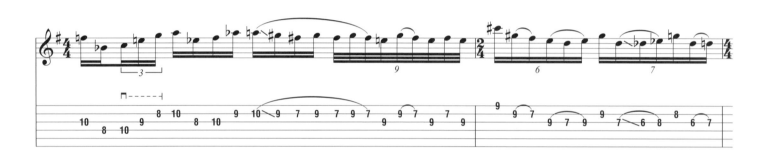

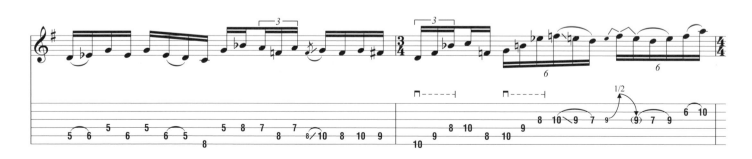

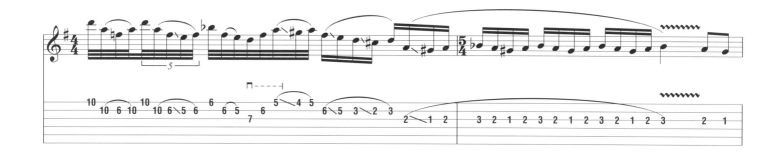

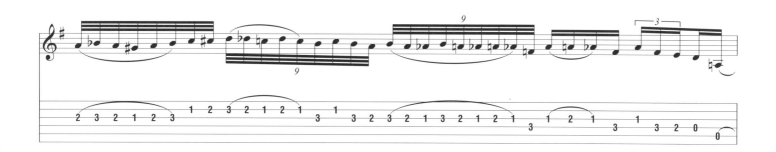

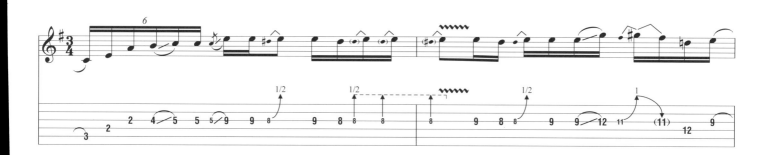

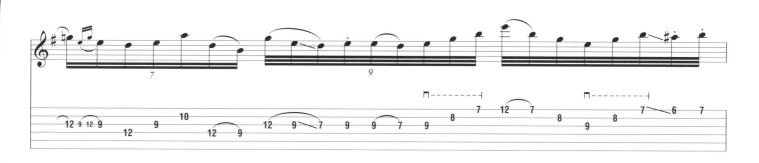

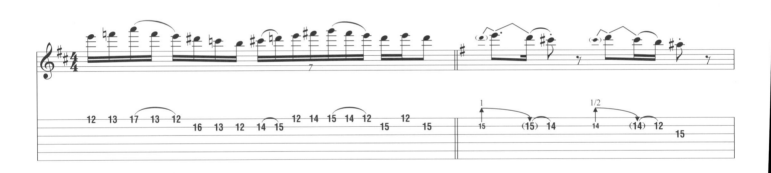

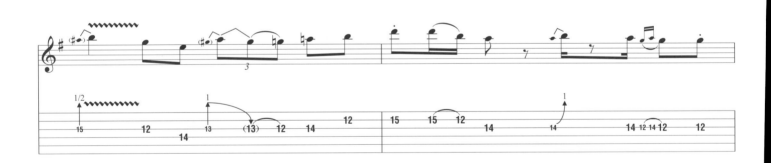